Give Me Room to Move My Feet

For my family
Your love unchangeable
throughout the ages.

Give Me Room to Move My Feet

Mildred Kiconco Barya

Published by Amalion Publishing 2009

Amalion Publishing
BP 5637 Dakar-Fann
Dakar CP 00004
Senegal

www.amalion.net

Copyright © Mildred Kiconco Barya, 2009

ISBN 978-2-35926-001-4 HB

ISBN 978-2-35926-002-1 PB

Author's photo © Martin Dixon

Cover designed by Will McCarty

Printed and bound in Great Britain by Antony Rowe, Chippenham, Wiltshire

All rights reserved. No part of this publication may be reproduced, transmitted, or stored in a retrieval system, in any form or by any means, without permission in writing from Amalion Publishing, nor be otherwise circulated in any form of binding or cover than that in which it is published

Contents

Revolving Lives

Existential Cycle 2
What We Leave 3
Living Out of a Suitcase 4
The Place Where You Begin (The Third World) 5
Way in, Way out 6
Beyond the Crossing 7
Skipping 8
Sea and Sky 9
The Perfect Match 10
Life's Wounded 11
The Look of Pain 12
Greeting Moon 13
What Are We Here For? 14
I Shall Ask Grandma to Write Me a Recommendation 15
This Too Is Life 16
Where Do Street Kids Go When They Grow? 17
Street Intelligence 18
Faceless 20
November in Dakar 21
Escape 22
Travellers 23
Monday Mornings 24

Stormy Heart

Stormy Heart 26
Wash Down 28
Medical Conditions 29
The Last Ring 30
I Remember 31
Decorum 32
Familiar 33
Is this life? 35

Scarred 36
Tell Me 37
Things That Melt Us 38
If I Was 39
Favourite Verb 40

Before the Sun Sinks

At the River's Edge 42
Farewell Song 44
Miracle Inside 45
The Feeling 47
Faraway 48
Grandma and I 49
A Fragile Moment 50
The Element We Become 51
Before the Sun Sinks 52
To My Sister with Laughter in Her Eyes 53
At the River's Bend 54
Sipi 55

The Pain of Tenderness

Nectar 58
The Moon Keepers 59
The Pain of Tenderness 60
Grilled Pain 61
Smooth Fade 62
A Wish 63
Sick Heart 64
Switchboard 65
We Made Love in the Rain 66
Elements of Love 67
Dream Carriers 68
Dear Trevor 69
Africa so Same 70

Shame Has a Place

Revolutionaries 72
Seth Africa 74
They Could Have 75

What's Native Can't Harm You	76
Thisblessedcontinent	77
When I See Bleeding Hearts	78
Soon	79
Thief	80
Dead End	81
Just So You Know	82
When We Fall	83
Ice and Fire	84
The Divided Falls	85

The Shape of Dreams

The Call	88
For the Legend	89
Walking into the Den	90
Heaven	91
Prayers and Promises	92
Popenguine	93
Mender of the Broken	94
Wish	95
Prints	96
The Dreamers	97
On this Mount Elgon	98
Drink of the Deep	99
The Clarifier	101

Until the Last Breath Is Drawn

Ears	104
God's Fool	105
Parting	106
Waiting	107
The Great Saver	108
Seeds of His time	109
Coexistence	110
A Little Balance	112
Africa Remains	113
Being People	114
We Are Not Dealing with Fractions	115
God and Man	116

Acknowledgements

TrustAfrica. I appreciate you for believing. For giving me enough room to dream, to write this collection during my time as Writer in Residence. Special mention goes to Akwasi Aidoo and Jeanne Elone. You have continually fuelled my creative pursuits. Without you words would be a desert and my pages so dry.

Per Ankh establishment. For teaching me what matters. Ayi Kwei Armah, my mentor and midwife, I salute you. You filled my gourd with beautiful thoughts.

My friend, Aissatou Ka. You know more than you can tell. You have kept me sane.

My beautiful souls: Karima Grant, Jackee Batanda, Goretti Kyomuhendo, Sandra Okoed, Amani Gueye, Susan Kiguli and Beverley Nambozo. You constantly hold my candle. You do not give up on me. Because of you my star shines.

My family. Your names are not written here. They are imprints on my heart. I honour you with the ink of these poems.

Thomas J. Haslam, for arriving on time.

My publisher, Amalion, for an important step of trust and collaboration.

Thank you.
MK Barya.

Revolving Lives

Existential Cycle

Do you realise everything moves,
Everything happens,
Everything is nothing?

Do you *not see* nothing happens?

Do you realise nothing moves,
Nothing ends,
Everything ends?
*

What We Leave

Here we are, again,
revolving in an inescapable circle
sometimes starting in the middle
to the end and the beginning

often we are trapped
we neither progress nor regress
nor do we fall sideways
stagnant matter in a torporific state
netted in a zone of waiting

then the spinning

it seems to me
we always go back
to what we leave
life's residues are not dregs
to be thrown away
the cliché is right after all —
it's not over until it's over

so we find ourselves on the move
return to who we are, what we are
it matters no more.

some day we will talk of a time and place
like here where we are
where we have been
where we are going and where we return.
*

Living Out of a Suitcase

For Emily Simon in San Francisco

She talks of living with
Eight families or so
In a three-month span.
To move out on her own
She needs a steady pay check.

She says there,
Like here,
You must know
Someone large
Who can fix you
You may not engage your brain.

Soon you realise
A painful trade-off
Creativity, originality, freewill…
Even robots today have thoughts and will.

And humans?
Lives in motion
With no place they are really going to or coming from
And many cops on the streets.

*

The Place Where You Begin (The Third World)

Everyone calls us Third World
Including our children,
It seems so much the First
A place where you make a clean start
Where you begin afresh.

It is true we were disorganised
Plagued with basic lacks and wants
Regular electricity, flowing water, a little hygiene
We must gather momentum to transpose
To a higher key – the Second World
Where we can afford bread and butter
Pay exorbitant taxes
Send our children to school.
Life spins on a complex fast forward,
Lacking sophistication.

The Third World is best
You can get a million things done
Seated in one place
Press a switch, type in a password
The choice of transaction is yours,
Fall in love. Watch a movie. Open a shop. Bank on line.
Ideal to some,
Excessive to the modest, wanton extravagance.
To the travellers it is worth exploring,
To the goal setters worth reaching,
To the dreamer it is reality.

Everyone calls us Third World
Including our children.
*

Way in, Way out

Sometimes, the only way out
Is a break from the familiar
To review contents of the dream bag
When the life you know sucks.

Sometimes
Out
Is the only way in
Growing younger as you age
Stronger and mellow like oak wine.

Not everyone who keeps moving is restless
Not all who stay in one place are anchored.
Sometimes stability is in mobility
The only way in,
The only way out.
*

Beyond the Crossing

We've come to the core
We'll disband
Embrace vicissitude
I'll not restrain you
From walking away
Don't turn to watch me go.

All our life here
Will root elsewhere
Love has become bohemian, to have thought
Our souls were here
Our similar path.

Our feet will journey on
Energised by individual sense of reality
Under a blanket of night
Beyond the crossing
Tempted to cast our eyes back.
*

Skipping

People believe our creator blesses other generations
and skips theirs.
Our parents were the blessed lot. They loved whole,
married well.
We are the skipped.
Our loves gone sour, nations betrayed at our hands,
Justice ripped from her seat.
Where hearts should have been we carry fragments
Everything we have touched has broken, is left un-mended
We spin in unknown directions without destination
Without occupation, without a country
At the final hour the joy of the journey dries up
We are more troubled than before
We cannot tell in whose territory is favour
But once we've passed on like a discord in a song
Those after us will think we were the chosen
And they
The skipped.
*

Sea and Sky

Clouds of kisses
Billow up and cover sky
Waves of love
Roll and sweep over sea
Sea and sky dance
Giving each other colour
The half moon cheers on
With her split smile.
*

The Perfect Match

I.
She quarrels with her man
because he likes to cook,
he knows how.

II.
She does all the chores
her man can't boil an egg,
or find his socks.

I.
She threatens to divorce because
he picks up the laundry, empties the bin
and attends family planning sessions.

II.
He has burnt her certificates
he demands she remains home
knitting shawls and breeding kids.

I.
He brings her the job pages
so she may try her luck
she prefers staying home watching TV.

II.
He points fingers and picks up an axe
children take cover under the beds
she flees to the cattle shed.
*

Life's Wounded

You see them,
You can hear their pain echo day after day,
Life's wounded.

Beyond affluent estates they wear
Life's harshest scars
Flicking through life magazines and TV channels
Cuddled with books on the sofa,
Fighting demons that come with insomnia.

They drive big fancy cars
Raise clouds of dust in their haste to nowhere
Their language is credit cards, holidays abroad…
Their eyes suffused with old and new wounds.
*

The Look of Pain

You can always see the look of pain whichever spot you stand
In the empty eyes of children huddled on the streets,
In the familiar heartache songs you hear,
In the frenzied beats of the drums,
In the wounds that pound with a rhythmic echo,
Universal pain.

We fear to touch it
We are afraid how it exposes us
If only we knew we own it
As much as those who bear it
It would make us whole.

You can always hear the look of pain no matter how far you stand
The sound of her heart cracking,
The creaking rope hanging in the barn,
The tale of the elders whose land is stolen,
The dreams of the young smashed against rocks,
The wails of those seeking a rest,
Hope and home.

We fear to touch it
If only we knew we own it
As much as those who bear it
We would be whole.
*

Greeting Moon

The night is seductive
Come.
The green trees will be our shade
As we watch this sacred birth.

Head first
She peeps out
Her day in our night.

Now she's following us
Wherever we move
On her first day.

There she is ripe, round
Soon it will be farewell
Death and dawn.
*

What Are We Here For?

Now there's a tune ringing
Sometime
I won't remember what I am singing

What am I here for?

There's a code to knowledge of our ancestors
Sometime
We won't pass on our heritage

What are we here for?

There are symbols to ways of our forerunners
Sometime
We won't decipher the texts

How shall we know who we are?
*

I Shall Ask Grandma to Write Me a Recommendation

The scholarship office
States the requirement before admission:
A letter of recommendation from a higher faculty
Familiar with my work;
A tutor, a mentor, who has seen my progress over time
With a smirk on my face
I run to Grandma.

Years gone
We sat under the big eucalyptus tree
Surrounded by pine trees in our compound
She chronicled Histories and Herstories
Dating centuries back

She explained the mysteries woven in our beads
Ancient journeys of our people in our names
Tracking generations forward and rearward

She narrated folk tales
Embedded with morals and vices too
How the kingdom of monsters and humans relate.

The tales she told are the stories I write
The first time I showed the Professor my work,
'This can't be you,' he bellowed.
'This shows years of practice and genius,
Whose are these?'

I told Grandma who understood it all
'It looks to me your professor is a mediocre,' she said.

I shall ask her to write me a recommendation letter
I shall ask Grandma to mail her letter to the scholarship office.
*

This Too Is Life

The taxi gives up the ghost
In the middle of nowhere
Something's faulty with the gearbox
And only one door can open to let us out
Apart from the licence which hasn't expired,
Our driver doesn't have a permit
He's been at the wheel all his life
Get what I mean?

We come across people with beaming faces
Grinning wider than the sea
A loud cry pierces the air
We run to rescue the endangered species
A woman is giving birth all by herself
A pair of twins in this wilderness, in the end
We clap and sing as the men sound the big drums

We make camp and start a fire
We sit in a circle and clear our throats
There are good storytellers here
Who talk of a country without fuel crises
A before that was pure and fresh
Now it's useless to dream
Our car is evidence of what's lost
Those worn-out tyres carrying our life
And children's scribble on the dust-coated windshield,
'Clean Me, Please.'

It is clear we've abandoned our journey
I complain how we are missing our life beyond
We need to repair the car, find fuel and move on
My friends say in the most relaxed way,
This too is life.
*

Where Do Street Kids Go When They Grow?

Where do street kids go when they grow?
When they turn into men and women
Where do they go?

Hundreds of children walking the streets,
Begging for bread,
Where do they go?

We ignore them and think they're lucky to get
A few coins that we toss
When they grow and dress another part
And say, 'Maam, Sir,' in a gentle tone,
What happens?

If you knew they have proposed to
Your daughter, your son
Would you gather energy to bless?

Have you wondered
Why your child-in-law,
Tells nothing of the foundation years?

All their lives they told a story
Now they're silent men and women
Do you hear how loud their story?
*

Street Intelligence

Even the beggar must purchase the tin that holds the coin
And he's clever enough to put away the paper money
Or else he loses his niche
If only you were here I would tell you I finally agree
There are many things they never teach in school
We are much safer learning them somehow.

I thought you would wait
To watch your dreams on the canvas
Your name at the bookends
And long lines watching your right hand
Autograph a million copies
You had more spine, ambition
Still you had to go.

You started that continent-saving-campaign
Got a large following
But it's you who needed saving
Those peace cards you had us sign,
I would like to tell you more nations are now at war,
And it has got nothing to do with skin.

You should be here
Swallowing espresso and screwing up your nose
Swearing on your coffee breath
Writing commentaries and theories on street intelligence

In the very lake you learnt how to swim,
They have discovered wells of oil-sparking ethnic clashes
Each kingdom claiming a piece of the water body
The peacekeepers are hovering
Dropping bombs and laying their bases

We have become the 'special focus' in the news
A lot they don't teach in school,
I will tell you.
*

Faceless

Drink the tears in your eyes
Disappear in the crowds
Take a trip out of this life
Travel and travel

> Let's go faceless
> We are the tough crew
> Who should see us breaking
> When we can go faceless?

Those once upon a time forget-me-nots
Hide them, hide them
And the pain in your heart
The hunger in her eyes

But when we hear
Sighing of those who are waiting
How can we pretend all is well?
Won't we stretch our hands and touch them
To see the smiles beyond their desperate stares?

> Then we can't go faceless
> As the tough crew
> Fearing breaking
> No we can't go faceless.
> *

November in Dakar

The Harmattan is here
Blowing hot dust in our faces
It's useless taking shield
Let it pass
Let it be.

Our skin turns into fish scales
Our lips chapped like crocodile hide
Our eyes teary from allergies
Noses rock with sneezing spells.

At last
The sun withdraws her fangs
Nights turn cool
Couples get closer
Welcoming the change.
*

Escape

Escape
Is what we look for
When the familiar no longer holds

Escape
Is what we utter
When our dreams have miscarried

Escape
Is what we seek
When exiles are forced upon us

Escape
Is what we find
When we turn our backs on each other.
*

Travellers

'Shit happens',
that's what my friend Sam says
when trouble spills to his space

sometimes fleeing is the thing,
not merely stepping away.

In another twist
he will go through the challenge
in the name of 'the obstacle is the path',
baptisms of rational sense here and there,
then and now.

He thinks we are some kind of travellers
where are we going?
where are we coming from?

Still i admit he surprises me with
poetry lines walking out of his head
i write them down lest i forget
some day when i cannot confront my own demons
and i'm pacing, he drops one of them:
'Seekers will be restless when they feel a sense of nothing.'
i pretend he's not talking to me
but the shape gets clearer with his next line:

'Pay attention to the pathway,
not the future, not the past'.
it's one of his ways of grounding me
to his face only i say he's stuck in a journey.
*

Monday Mornings

Monday mornings
Like life
Are never easy
They come with a lot of indigestion,
Constipation, exhaustion,
Hang-ups and hangovers.

We rejoice when it turns out a public holiday
Then we can extend the weekend
Or when nature an expert on suffering
Calls attention to herself,
Suddenly the roads are impassable
Thunder fells the power lines
Lame structures are washed away
Normal routine disrupted.

It's a gift,
If it happens early Monday morning
And you still have a roof, a bed, and good coffee
You snuggle within your safe skin
Embrace the rest a good Monday brings.
*

Stormy Heart

Stormy Heart

A heart like mine
Fickle,
But generous
I welcome him,
Them
We are us.

Shades start to peel
Revealing who they are
Masqueraders.
Once more,
I've been deceived.

There are many
Coming through my open door
My sister advises
I should have a selection method
Tight and soundproof
But that way, I tell her
I might block the real thing
Cut the oxygen to my heart
What if there's nothing left of a heart?
I see splinters.

Another time a friend asks,
Have I any children?
'No.'
'I am sure there have been men.'
'So?'
'At your age they've given you no children?'
'They've given me principles,'
He laughs,

I tell him there's another thing,
Absent fathers
Missing husbands
Lone mothers
There are too many.

Now I am seated by the ocean
Wind roars,
Waves roll and rock with the shore
Turbulence swells
Just like it is
With my stormy heart.

*

Wash Down

I am where we saw each other first
I'd be expectant if these were normal circumstances

Carrying a thick brown envelope
He spills on the table gifts I 've sent him
I do not take back what I've given.
"Pride", he hisses.

A smiling waitress comes
Glances at the pictures, presents
"What would you like to have, madam?"
Black coffee, strong like death.
"Yes, maam. And you?"
A milk shake.

We've been compatible
Until the magnified orders
Brokenness like loss
Reveals the truth too late
He prefers White, me Black.
Coffee sips, the colour of Guinness twice bitter
Scalds my tongue, reaches where
The slicing knife is lodged.

I would come here again,
For a package of bad news
To wash down with dark coffee.
*

Medical Conditions

Love
    Pain
Jealousy
    Anger
Are medical conditions
To be assuaged with homeotherapy and
Grandma remedies.

Otherwise
Why am I here
In the mute night
Grinding ginger
Infusing mint tea
Concocting chicken soup
Soaking my feet in dead-sea salts
Scrubbing at tired conversations.
*

The Last Ring

The phone should ring
Should have rung
A while ago.

Days, weeks, months
I sit here knowing
The phone should ring any minute.

Days, weeks, months
I notice a ring of grey
And throw away the ring.
*

I Remember

I remember
Forgetting you.
Why do you appear
Now?
Why do I see your face
Now?
We never stop loving
Those we have loved fiercely
Possessively
I remember you.
*

Decorum

It's the least we could do,
Holding hands
Saying *Merci*
Thinking what we could be.

It's the least we could do,
Watching movies
Running in the rain
Reading poetry by the moonlight.

It's the least we could do,
Exchanging texts beyond hours
Talking of 'we,'
Might be.

It's the least we could do,
Washing our feet in the river
Massaging each other's back
Asking at the bus park, 'Have we said all?'

It's the least we could do,
Spending time together,
Denying.
*

Familiar

I've been on the run,
Again.

You won't let me
Play hide and seek
You know it's fun.

The reason I am before you today
Is for us to strike some kind of deal
Lord, since you're older than I
You have experience
Point towards the direction
The rest of the way I will figure it out
Wait a minute, dear Lord,
It's so dark
Shine a little and we'll be okay.

Good grief
There are sharp stones in my path,
Now you're by my side
Careful, Lord,
We might hurt ourselves
Hmm,
You carry me?

'Child, these are my familiar paths.'

Your eyes,
That painful expression in your eyes,

'It's all right child,'

You soothe me?

Is it me or you crying?
Hot tears. I cannot see.
Oh, Lord.

"Shh, I am with you, always."

Why do you put up with me?

"I am and you are not,
Someday,
You will
Be."
*

Is this life?

I have been talking to you
I hear your echo like you're miles away

Is this life?

We know things that make us older
In one night we age

Is this life?
*

Scarred

He came to my door
With many scars and much baggage
I would have taken him in if he were light
Where would I place his load?

Sadly he walked away
Bowed by the weight of his burden
I swear I wanted to help him
If he wasn't carrying his past.

He was stamped there
A part of the wastelands
He wouldn't let go
He was rooted there.

You know the feeling
When one day help is limited
I would have given him a hand
If he wasn't stuck in the past.

He clutched
Splinters of broken years
He wouldn't let go
He was fixed there.
*

Tell Me

If I were a River
Carrying loads,
Would you accept me?

If I led you to the Source
And you drank water cupped in my hands,
Would that satisfy you?

If I were Earth
To plough and harvest,
Would that nourish you?

If I were a Fire
Radiant in your dreams
Consuming the world,
Would it appease you?
Endear me to you?

Tell me.
*

Things That Melt Us

I hear it from the next room
The sound of his steady hand stirring sugar in his tea
Like he's ringing a bell
With such energy one could put to greater use
But I am under the veil
I only listen to my heart singing,
Wanting and waiting.

On another day it's a call he answers
The laughter in his voice tingles my skin
His warmth penetrates the wall
He laughs so well like an ocean rising, lapping the shore.

His humming is another thing,
Lots of Earth songs, he's well grounded
He sure makes my soul fly,
I want to see his face.

I tell my sister I'm in love
Who is the fella? Her eyes glow for a story
As far as truth is truth, there is none.
She probes, thinking I'm playing a game,
I give her the little I know
Is he single?
Who knows
Is he available?
Who can tell
How did you meet?
We haven't met,
Wait this evening
You will hear him come home
Then you'll know for sure what I am talking about
She gives me the sorry-you're-crazy-my-sister-look.

If I Was

If I was a dancer,
My steps would lead me to you.

If I was a landscaper,
I would sketch living colours in your name.

If I was an interior designer,
I would spread decorations of my dreams for you.

But I am a dark poet
Too stiff to dance
Apprehensive to stretch a rainbow to see
Beyond the furnishings of this mental-scape.
*

Favourite Verb

Stay is a nice word
Kinder than most verbs I know
It's like ice in warm hands,
A fragrant scent in a room
A glowing fire on a cold night.

Stay is a dangerous word
Disarming than most weapons I know
A bomb in skilled hands
A drug to an addict
The fury of the sun.
*

Before the Sun Sinks

At the River's Edge

For all those supporting people living with HIV/AIDS

The neutral observer on the fence
Looks neither left nor right
Let the cats fly
Let sleeping foxes lie
Hands folded on the chest
Folks die one by one
Children are forced to head homes.

Across the road
We hear their laughter like the song of rivers
We are moved to join them
We take the step to say sorry
Our eyes on the camera we come full circle
We tell our troubles and it helps
We do not blame, we do not condemn
Our voices rise in one language:
Daughter, Son of Africa
Reach out.

We touch each other, tender
We take turns to care for the sick
And prepare to let them go each day
Ghost-like before the drug
We choose to be resilient, not resigned
We can do anything
Mine tunes out of rocks
Print our tears on the wall of shame
Our hallmark of courage
Our brothers and sisters go through the fire
Dying, and we sing to them.

Strands of life in which we are woven reel on
Birds with broken wings
Sweeter melodies to bring
When we stand at the edge of the river
We are each other's bridge
To cross and to return.
*

Farewell Song

When I am gone,
Think of me flowing freely,
Running deep,
Swelling and echoing across the centuries,
Irrigating desert plains,
Nurturing plants on your shore.

When I am finished with my years
Don't think of me as a wilderness
Growing thorns,
Trampled upon,
I will remain your fertile ground, yielding,
Bringing fruits to your store.

When I am no more
I will not hoard like a reservoir,
I will not hold back,
I will give generously,
I will sustain you.
*

Miracle Inside

I sit in the chapel trying to make sense
Of the white-washed walls
Why the heart cannot be that clean
Why the spirit must keep seeking

There's a big crack through the plaster
I think about the foundation, the bricks
The waterproof roofing
Bats have nests in the ceiling
The pastor's words stolen

I look for the face of Jesus
Hands cup my cheeks
Lips touch my skin and breathe on me
A kiss so refreshing, unadulterated
Tears run down
It's sweet to cry
This visitation of mercy
The stone inside me melts.

I walk out of the chapel larger than vastness
The preacher is concluding his sermon
I do not wait on the steps outside
To hear about last Sunday's collection
I am carrying the benediction
When I reach home, I make a pyre
For the management books I've feverishly purchased
Anti-depressants, anti-stressors, how's and be's
To deal with the wrongness out there
I stand on the staircase
Watch them burn.

Doors open
I am surrounded
I hear voices. Is she okay?
It's Jesus. He's given me new life.
At the mention of Jesus some walk away
She has lost it, they say,
Looking at me with pity in their eyes
He's come to me. It's Jesus, louder this time.
I think we'll have to take her away
The Chairman of the area says
Losing no time I spring into my room
Securely shut the door,
Holding the miracle inside.
*

The Feeling

Bring back the feeling
When we were grateful
For so little provided.

Bring back that feeling
When we rejoiced for what we had
And that which we didn't know we lacked.

Bring back the feeling
When we loved all that we were
All that we would never be.

Dear Lord, take back the feeling
That make us ache
For what we didn't know we could have been
All that we should have been but were not.
*

Faraway

There she stands in his eyes
She thinks she can help him
She says she can lead him,

Faraway
Faraway

He drinks water cupped in her hands
From springs at the foot of the mountains
In the deserts of Africa,

Faraway
Faraway

There she is again in his eyes
If he can know her name
She can lead him,

Faraway
Faraway.
*

Grandma and I

We are shelling peas on a reed mat on the veranda
The sky is clothed in variant shades of blue
A few dark clouds scatter in circular motions
Whispers of wind are rhythmically trapped
And released in the eucalyptus branches
The river keeps on rolling
It's hard to believe a few minutes ago
Heavy rain was here
It has left its smell on the leaves
On my breath, on the damp soil.
Now there's a drizzle and sun in conversation
This is the moment our ancestors called hyena's wedding
When rain drops and sun shines at the same time
I love it here
To sit serenely with Grandma
Leave sound to our hands cracking pods
Soaking in the seasons' beauty.
In a little while
The sun will disappear
Wrapped in an orange and purple hue
Grandma will say, 'Daughter of Sunset,
It's time to get in the house.'
Soon the holiday will be over
I will return to the city
Where no stars are seen in the night,
No firefly glow,
And there's no Grandma,
Daughter of Earth.
*

A Fragile Moment

He talks to me
Of his confusion
The fight for faith
Pain hidden in the changing seasons.

He removes his skin
So I can touch him tender
Cuddle the baby in him
Not the macho man on parade.

I have witnessed all kinds of departure
I have endured uncertainties of waiting
But this moment I hold on to myself,
Until the fragility passes.
*

The Element We Become

I come clanging in copper bracelets
Jingling my gold anklets
Eyes twinkling
Ears flashing polished diamond stones
My quicksilver smile shimmering
A band of rubies falling on my neck.

You appear dressed in fire
Your dark oiled skin a lustrous sheen

My smooth skin rubbed with ochre
Adorned with henna
A riot of colourful beads
Rising to the rhythm of my shaking waist.

We do our dance
Our feet light as wind
Our pulsating bodies one river
Flowing and flooding the bank
Skin in skin
Heart in heart
And Earth listening to the element we become.
*

Before the Sun Sinks

Before the sun sinks
I shall go to the river
Find a rock to sit my soul
Place my feet in the waters.

Before the sun sinks
I shall play my thumb piano
Sing songs of my mentors
Compose new notes for tomorrow.

Before the sun sinks
I shall make love
Let go of sorrow
Release shadows of torn countries and lost heritage.
*

To My Sister with Laughter in Her Eyes

For Maimouna

You sing many poems
And love to dance in the night
You once lived near the lake
And journeyed to the desert
Here's my story as I have watched you grow.

They like to smear dung in your yard
And turn your name to shame
'We have broken her,' they hiss
You who love to rise with the sun.

They may jeer and turn their noses up as you pass
They will drop all sorts of hints
Nothing you do will please them, satisfy them
Stay on steady, daughter of twilight.

They will talk before and behind your back
Anticipate your resignation
Sister, jiggle your shoulders and toss wine
Or celebrate with a bowl of vegetables.

Wear your pride and race ahead
Gallop with the horses without weariness
And when you've crossed to the shore
Lay down gracefully and glow
Daughter of dawn.
*

At the River's Bend

We stop
Hesitant to proceed

We look neither left nor right
We're in focus with the crow

Yet we do not move straight ahead
We wait

Mosquitoes come
Out of the swamps

Kiwi birds flap their wings
To return home

Our eyes stop at the bend
So does the river flow.
*

Sipi

What have you in common with the ancient Mississippi
That your name should be hewn out of that river?
Perhaps it's the beauty you share, immense
Long with endurance, swollen with stories
Formidable. Imposing.

To drink from your wellness
A traveller can never forget
Cool, refreshing you are
You're here forever.

Many come round
To watch you,
Drink of you
Deep.

Sipi

You satisfy.
What have you
In common with that river
That mighty winding river
In a country so far, far away?
You are loud, wild in your falls
Decreasing boulders to fragments
You are beautiful, harsh, and ferocious,
Sipi, what have you in common with that river,
That long Mother of a river in a country far away?

*

The Pain of Tenderness

Nectar

Back in your arms
When life was nectar
We drank it up
Do you ever recall those moments?

We were notes in a song
Our voices creating chords
Our bodies the harmony
Do you still hear echoes of our rhythm?

Back in our days
It was dangerous a love like ours
We couldn't live it up
Do you share my regret?

Our pounding hearts
Welcoming the softness of rain
A thousand kisses on a feathered bed
How could we give it up?
*

The Moon Keepers

We watched the moon
A boy carrying a baby
You saw six pigs.

On another night a sad old woman
You said it was an old man
It did not stop us from being.

Some nights we saw the same
We looked up the world mapped there
An old couple ageing gracefully
The woman chewing tobacco
The old man smoking a pipe
Their hands on each other's lap
We called them the moon keepers.

Beyond memory reach
Each tradition sees in the moon
A part of themselves and belief
We hoped some generation would see us.

When did we begin to lose saneness?

We gaze
At the moon
Hanging firmly
On the roof of the sky
It's just an empty moon
We had become the moon keepers
When did we leave our place?

The Pain of Tenderness

Each visitation to a place you've once been
Once loved, recalls luggage carried and
Much left behind, packaged
In suitcases of sad times.

Some scenes are worth a repeat
Parts of a landscape indelibly etched
On your map
Dots, lines, contours of people
Lakes and rivers of events
Moments there.

When you cannot face them without an itch
A powerless desire to scratch the scar
To stare, to touch, to feel and remove
The protective crust
To re-own the boiling sensation
To lose yourself once more
I'll tell you why
It's the pain of too much tenderness.
*

Grilled Pain

Sometimes
Pain is not what hurts most
But desire

Sometimes
Sadness is not as heavy
As emptiness

You should know
Loss isn't bad
Longing is

Now you know
Restlessness doesn't kill
Deferred hope does.
*

Smooth Fade

This fading
into nothing
do you feel it?

I'd rather we crashed
like cymbals struck
thunder tearing
kente cloth ripping.

Not this smooth fade
like cinema lights dimming.

Pick your odor
from my bed
bring back the keys
take me instead

I remind me of you.
*

A Wish

I
wish
depression
had
a
cure.

*

Sick Heart

We have been talking
Touching the way lovers do.

Your departure
Leaves a sour taste in my mouth.

Separation, you say,
Puts bile on your tongue.

Thoughts of you, me,
Fill us with yearning ache

Here we beg at the doctor's clinic
Wanting to cure the sick feeling
We'll do all except admit
Winds of love blowing our way.
*

Switchboard

Love should have been a rock
A boulder or a bump of granite
We wouldn't feel much pain
When it's over.

Love should have been a musical note
A character in songs for quality or mood
We wouldn't cry
When the songs end.

Love should have been an abstraction
Pigs in heaven or the man on the moon
We wouldn't be devastated
When we hold divergent conceptions.

Love should have been a condition
Treatable with a prescribed dose
We wouldn't be dysfunctional
When we notice the symptoms.

It's a touch, a look, a beautiful thought
A person or a thing
A name on a plain page
Hard to confine to a switchboard.
*

We Made Love in the Rain

We made love in the rain
The drops we could catch
The drops we let fall
Were our hearts.

Words should be dead or else
How can we talk again,
See each other,
When we live dead to love?

This void, this numbness,
Do you feel it?
The dizziness overcoming the senses,
How could we choose the desert over rain?
*

Elements of Love

If I were Wind
Trapped in your trees
Would that move you
To come to me?

If I were Earth
Sprawled for you
Would you lie down
And embrace me?

If I were a River
Flowing to your yard
Would you drink from me
To cool your thirst?

If I were a Fire
Glowing in your hearth
Would you draw closer
To keep warm?
*

Dream Carriers

How does it feel
to watch a future slip from your reach?

Is it like losing ground in a job interview
breaking you in cold sweat?

Is it like the thrash of a harmattan wind
whipping desert sand in your face?

Or it's like stabbing an open sore
whose pounding pain is deeper than the wound itself?

Is it like a headache whose splitting effect
spreads to the toes?

How does it feel to watch your dreams
slip from your reach?
*

Dear Trevor

You were for peace
Violence claimed you
You were pro-life
Death walked through the front door
And twisted you out of shape
Your mangled body made us weep
Perhaps not because you had gone
But how it happened

We've talked with friends left
How you walked among us
Your warmth, your generosity
Your readiness to help
You had much to live for
How could you die?

Tell me how to lay down the pain
To watch you go
And nod with the saying, 'the good die young.'
I will not pretend, 'Oh death, where is your sting?'
It's right here, a poison arrow in our flesh.

Earth couldn't keep you safe
I believe heaven will
I am hoping for a sign
Now you're beyond harm's way
Then, only then will I know
Someday we'll see each other again
And laugh at death in the face.
*

Africa so Same

Here I am
Bags and all
From Africa
Into deep Africa

A small yellow-dotted taxi comes
There's no door to close
Windows do not open
Roads are punctuated with potholes
On both sides of the street
Children beg.

My hosts are apologetic
Generous with laughter and tears
It makes me want to cry
Seeing Africa so same.

I am home
It is all so familiar
It makes me want to weep
Seeing Africa so same.
*

Shame Has a Place

Revolutionaries

Remember our political study group
We were young, naïve and intelligent
Martyrs to renounce our lives
Believed we could save Africa
How I laugh to remember.

We marched to the Congo
Ready to die heroes
Before the Rwandan genocide became
'Rwigyema,' we cried
'Freedom here we come!'

Soon the Darfur crisis summoned us
We could have gone on in reckless ambition
But we had pledged our weapons
Wouldn't only be physical
Did our commanders believe in thinking, thinkers?

One by one
Our colleagues died
But the government denied the deaths
We saw how cheap we were
'It's only peace that we want,' they said
All they approved were senseless wars
Our bosses got fat on the gold
Slept under mosquito nets in the best hotels
While we shared the bush with snakes and spiders

We woke up finally
To gather what was left of us
We picked up our squashed dreams
Every step of our return journey
Reverberated with the heaviness of loss.

The continent wastes on
We are home trying out new skins
How could they feed us lies?
How easy it was to trust
Oh, comrade, how I die to remember.
*

Seth Africa

We were not permitted in our country
When the seal was broken finally
    We still require foreign papers to legalise our entry.

    Once we were not allowed home
    The white-man said with a sneer
Now the black man says with a grin.

Today we don't call it our country
No, they are not part of us
And they say we are not part of them

Shame.
*

They Could Have

They could have walked on water
Rearranged the clouds

They could have drunk up the sea
Become gods

They could have restored the world
Re-named history

They could have loved, lived
The way they began

Instead
They let go
Listened to the talk of others
Bargained with the moment
Lost the future.
*

What's Native Can't Harm You

Children of a polished citizen
Visit their grandmother upcountry
Their mother packs tinned foods and waffles
Alternative capsules for vitamins.

They arrive at rural greens
Ripe mangoes and oranges
Waiting for eager hands
The tangerines too have yellowed
The berries are bursting
But mother has warned sternly
Stay off the native.

Grandma urges they relish the gifts in season
They shake their heads.
'Hunger is going to kill you amidst plenty.'
They'll catch a fever if they eat this and that
'What's native never killed nobody,'
She's just a bag of old age, they whisper
What can she know?

They open their large bags
Eat high-protein biscuits and chocolates
Swallow capsules
Run around the yard and play and sweat
But turn out stunted like fishermen's hooks.
*

Thisblessedcontinent

Worms wriggle in her curvaceous body
Vultures poke at her smelly armpits
Blighted, we love her all the same.

Her present state is partly our fault
The white man's aggravated robbery our nadir
We like apathy, our apogee
Our filthy life an apology
Mixing issues in a cauldron of misplaced notions,
Sentiments and logic
We feel when we should think
We think when we should feel
And we choose no side
When we are to stand
We go right when we are to be neutral
Sit on the fence
Instead of taking the left turn
Shameful nakedness.

Daily we recreate horrors, new sores
Dress up the corrupted body
Colonised minds and bloated egos
Not keen on healing our wounds
Ours is a dangerous contentment
Treacherous want
With or without more raid from
Disguised philanthropic contingents
For thisblessedcontinent.
*

When I See Bleeding Hearts

Frankly i admit
i must be a moron,
retarded,
to ache at open sores,
hear people justifiably saying,
'Nothing was serious.'
boy, they've taken her to a mental institution
nothing was serious, right?

surely it must be some kind of mistake
the man you've been with
takes unplanned leave
to get his mind together
find a cure for lost concentration
nothing was serious, right?

i must be a clod
i don't have a clue
this nothing-was-serious-business
when i see red,
red bleeding hearts.
*

Soon

Soon you will not hear my name
You're absorbed in your video game.

Soon you will not notice me
You're eager to say goodbye.

Soon you won't remember me
The way you forget to stir your tea.

Soon you won't know I passed here
And you once called me dear.
*

Thief

Bring back sleep
You stole from my dreams

Return every article
You snatched from my lips

The nouns and verbs on my tongue
Whispered words and those unspoken

Return my accent
You English thief

Take back your language
I have my words.
*

Dead End

I see your green light doesn't signal the usual passage
Doesn't differ from the red and yellow
The path to you is heavily jammed.

I sit back taking my usual shot of coffee, reading
Constitutional walks as you go through the motions
Routines of the day.

One day all will be clear that nobody left the other
Our lights were nothing
But shadows at the terminal.
*

Just So You Know

I have chosen to bury you
Where the soil is rock hard
Devoid of rich black
Softness and redness.

When you turn
Your body will
Scratch against the granite
You will neither grow nor rest.

As for my heart
Which you've turned bitter,
Boy, I've used your penknife to
Open the jar lid on the coffee table.
That's where I have placed it.
I can watch it smoking and souring
And say, No,
That's not my heart.
*

When We Fall

Today
I skinned a vulture
And divided the meat
Among us.

Mother
Refused her share
Do you know what vultures feed on?
On us, I said.

We are food
For vultures hovering
Ready to swoop
When we fall.
*

Ice and Fire

How shall we start to talk about things
that won't hurt our eyes?

It's more than a point of view,
It's blood.
Please don't talk about gain or loss,
Indulgence, restraint,
Feeling or indifference,
After undoing what was and is,
Could and might, would and never be,
Which way do we go?
Which road do we take?

Our arms around each other,
We became gods and sat on the wind
The earth moved
Now the world has stopped at our feet
We can hear our heartbeats
The echo of what we cannot change
Brother and sister in love
Ice and fire
Diverging from the same womb

How shall we talk about things
that won't hurt our memory?
*

The Divided Falls

People of Kapchorwa have divided the Falls
Of hair-pin bends
Gentle sloping hills and rock caves.

They put up three entrances
A fee for one Fall, more for the second and third
Because they pour out to different courses
Is it money?

You still would have received the fiscal pat
Sipi, fiercely beautiful,
We would pay gladly to gaze at you,
To soak in your pleasures

Ferocious you, we're on your side
A dazzling performance needs no deception,
They didn't have to lacerate your skin,
To trade your soul,
For tourist greed.
*

# The Shape of Dreams

The Call

Come to the edge, he said
It's dangerous there, I answered
Come to the edge, he said
I might fall and break my bones
Come to the edge, he said
I did
He pushed me
And I flew.
*

For the Legend

His eyes describe a place where hope has been
Love fighting the fiercest battle
Hearts ripped apart
Raw redness revealed.

His walk chronicles loss
Carried over years
An emptiness that grows larger
Becoming a part of his skin.

His talk evokes ruin
Set for the pyre
To rise like a phoenix.
*

Walking into the Den

For FEMRITE

I've been following an inner song about us
Not all the words are clear and bright
They echo a special feeling
A connection, a celebration
A poem calling out, coming into space
Becoming writers.

We vary in age and shape
Though we dream the same dream
We hold the same quill
We learn to care, to encourage, not to tear
We muster hope to wait and to love
We do not fight alone
It's not the kind to go solo.

Our words rise to the air
A song in the rock, a birth in the desert
Midwives attending the baby
Weaving fabrics to lay our differences
Cheering one another,
Planting and harvesting.
*

Heaven

Heaven is a bridge
Where two hearts come together as one.

Heaven is a site
Where flawed clay meets the porter.

Heaven is a point
Where hate and indifference melt.

Heaven is all around us
Yet we wear thick blinds to feel to see.
*

Prayers and Promises

I gave you a poem for all your watchfulness

You sent me a prayer for all my unbelief

I packaged my promises to match your dreams

You showed me pictures of all we could be

Is that all?
*

Popenguine

For Ayi Kwei Armah

There's something sacred and bird-like
The catholic would say it's the pope in the name
The free would say it's the penguin
There is release in this place
We are grouped together in the house of life
Building skeletons while flesh takes form.

We read books, swim and fly
We learn phrases in hieroglyphs
There's a seduction in that language
Like the lure of a baby's smile,
Like an old man's open door, inviting.

We become voyagers
Creating words from ocean waves
Humming tunes out of wind
At dawn we rise with the sun on the rock
At dusk we watch the sun sink into the sea.

Night opens her gate, crafting continues
Each finds a part to play
Watching, thinking, living, loving
Swinging in the hammock
Unfolding patterns of dreams
In the arms of Per Ankh.
*

Mender of the Broken

Together is where we should be
Help me stray to you
My hope, my promise
Defender of my dreams.

Show me how to mind you
Lead me where you are
Mender of the broken
Help me trust you.

Steady this moment
My unsure steps on the road
The future we make
Lover of me.

Possibility blooms
Let's gather pollen grains
Make nectar
Honey. Sweet. Filling.
*

Wish

Let's go anywhere, anywhere,
Let's go anywhere but here.

Let's roam, trek, journey
Let's travel anywhere, my dear.

Let's go now before the feet
Begin to question the mind.
*

Prints

From Tuks., October 2007

Daily
He creates beauty
Hangs it on my wall
Reflecting what's in his heart.

He opens his palms
Invites me to touch fabrics of
The future in the texture of his hands
I see patterns of the dream he dreams

Like a gift
Like a thought accompanying me on a solo trip
He stands. Watching. Waiting
Wanting me to hold the designs

In my days
Here and there and sometime beyond
There will be things I won't know by head or heart
But his prints I'll know, fashioned with strokes of love.
*

The Dreamers

Find us a river
That's gonna keep on rolling
Find us a sunset
Etched permanently on the horizon.

As we wrap our arms around each other
We will watch the continent sleep
Till the hours close the story
We will float and whisper in the trees
Like trapped sighing of waves.

We will rise in another place
Where words flow higher with the chant
Lovers love well
Singers sing well
And painters can paint us a picture
Of the loveliness we feel.
*

On this Mount Elgon

We could make every wish here
It would happen
In these high places near the sky
We are given wings
To be much more than we are
To be a future that we want
We could be anything here.

The moon hangs lazily
With her usual smile
Our heads are closer to the stars
The world can roll on
As we keep vigil with the stars.

We have flown and stroked mountain tops
We have embraced a vision of glory
Finally we know who we are
Responding to the wild
Drinking up the stream
The forests and the mountains
We are true.
*

Drink of the Deep

If we speak to the mass of these waters
Our laughter will rise
Compete with the howling sea, louder
Than the lapping of this ocean against the shore
Exhausted, we could lie on the folded waves and sleep.

Let's sing to the sky
And dream, leaving nothing to chance
We will ascend to the highest point
As we whisper *together* in the same breath

Shake-ups threaten to send us on
Solitary journeys
Fields call, the road turns,
Stalk and plant are one
How can we desert our hearts
For sweeping stereotypes confining us
To dissections of tradition, gender,
Religion, status, race…

Let's drink of the deep
Drums will roll on like thunder
As we give ourselves to the hurricane
Washing away tried conversations.

Embrace a connectedness our touch brings,
The hunger that melts us,
Makes us weak, mighty weak,
At this solemn hour.

Take together forward,
Have nothing to be ashamed of,
To look back over,
You mine, me yours.
Love, the noun and verb,
Moving us.

Let's break through like dawn,
Quicken the passing of dusk, together.
I will give you a walking dream
Let me hold you once more
Laugh with you across the table
Give me that smile that sets the whole night on fire.
*

The Clarifier

For David M

You've laboured to distinguish suits from shirtsleeves
Nothing substitutes for achievement
There's no harm determining power sources
Before running off in a whirlwind of determined energy.

It's okay to perfect one's ability
Walking confidently in direction of dreams
Rising well, consistently building a base
That's nearly unassailable.

Not all of us have to be architects of the blueprint
But we have a choice for spine and depth
To join in the excitement of creating futures.
*

Until the Last Breath Is Drawn

Ears

Mother used to shush us
'Walls have ears,'
In this IDP camp
There are no walls
Mother says
Fences can hear.

We are displaced here
But I ask
How can we be displaced?
No, thank you very much
We are placed here
Where there is a large fence and no walls.

We dig bunkers to dive in
When bombs go off
Loud and shattering like death
We do not open our lips
Everything here has ears.
*

God's Fool

They say
He's wasting time on God
God is not here, there.

He says
He'd rather be God's fool
Than man's guru

He will not bow to any standard
Judgement or touchstone
Cut by today's pacesetters.

Only God is his yardstick
He's happy to be God's tool
Content to be God's only fool.
*

Parting

The power of parting
Outweighs the intensity of love
Blood turning ice
You prepare to say goodbye.

A redeeming feeling in memory check
Not a thing wrong to love someone
To care, how sweet
To let go when that time comes.

Approaching the end, a warm ripple
Journeying through your body turns cold
Love-prints incised on your open-wounded heart.

You get weaker, become stronger
Die a little, layers of pain to fall
Bounce back so love is made perfect
In the most imperfect sense.
*

Waiting

It seems to me
Waiting is the wheel we spin on
Get the right pair of boots
A song to last the night.

The wick flickers, loyal to hope
Some things we've got to admit overstretch waiting
Babies born in camps grow to voting age
Without memory of a night of peace.

There are refugees trapped in a pause
Like a comma in the wrong place
Longing for a period of calm, a home
A future and a pathway
At the intersection of hope.

Between suspension and fulfilment stagnancy threatens
The optimistic, fatalistic, pessimistic, cynic lot
If it matters, matters not to hope
In the final transformation reel.
*

The Great Saver

We looked through guidebooks
To find the locus of the soul,
Meaning in our stars,
Defining personality.

We got clues from the career master
Shared our aspirations with him
I told my inner secret then,
To do everything to save the world
Higher calling beyond the ordinary.

Ladders of years
I am still in the same place
My feet have trodden virgin lands
They have known ancient paths
But I have not even saved my skin.

I have been talking with my sisters
Under the great saving illusion
'I am doing this for my country,
For my parents, for my constituency.'
I smile a knowing one and cheer, 'Go gals,'
Wait to hold them when the mirage clears.

It doesn't take long
We sit around the coffee table
Listening to the sound of frustration
Gathering splinters of our hearts:
'Africa needs no saving, neither the folks,
It's our fragile hearts in need of service,'
The bitterness of espresso lasts on our tongues
As we adjust our new lenses.
*

Seeds of His time

A farmer
>drops his seeds here and there
>>many to sprout
>breezes of heaven blow
and the rains come
>the seeds grow
>>fisted leaves turn lush green, unfold
the roots are firm, sucking nutrients from the soils
>fruits appear, large green
>>turning yellow with ripeness
>leaves change
>>fall back to the ground
>>>reminding us
>we are our creator's seeds
seeds of His time
>He feeds us,
nurtures us,
>that we may return to him someday
>>at the end of
>>>our season.

*

Coexistence

I
Living is a journey
You don't drink it up at once
Just like climbing Mt. Elgon
Each step is a phase. A tale.

II
The mountain shows and tells its story
Beginnings and growth
So we can trace ours
Learn a lesson for the future
Find a key for every door
Answers to questions unknown.

III
Nature sings welcome
The sound of water brushing against rocks
Wind whispering peace
Birds striking their first chorus
Singing to one another
Crickets lifting up their calypso
Hyenas laughing
Colobus monkeys swinging from tree to tree
Declaring this is their land.

IV
The cool breeze is here like a brother
And warm sunshine like a sister
If it were not for the cold nights
I would stay here forever
Touching rocks
Smelling flowers.

V

Around the campfire we are high
Telling the reasons we are here
Some to see the rare vegetation
Others to watch the sunrise on the rocks
Some to reach the peak
Life's travellers.

VI

Here is a peace that lasts
The memory we want to retain
Nature's postcard to us.

VII

On our last day we stop by a stream
To view our reflection, our dreams
Thunder reverberates in the rocks
Wind roars
Our fears rise in the heavy rain
The mountain sits on its elegant throne
We are humbled here
We learn to live together
With Mt. Elgon.
*

A Little Balance

I am a leaf
Losing pigment.

Wind whips me
I am fallen.

Is it possible
To perch on the branch again?

If someone tells me I can
I shall dance in the air
Glorify the tree that holds my roots.
*

Africa Remains

This continent is a witch
Without influence of any mortal
Her powers have nothing to do with humans.

We adore her in spite of afflictions
We want to be here, when we leave
We love to come back.

For centuries
Our goings and comings are a ceremony
But they are not about elephants and trees
Birds and the beads
No reference should be made
To drums and dance
Rivers and mountains

What brings us back
What makes us stay
Goes beyond Africa.
*

Being People

Words of silver
Turn into swords
Breaking hearts

Tongues lick the wound
Scar dry

Time steals our love
Trouble takes its toll
Till we give up

Routine numbs us
We grow silent
Age bends us
Tenderness breaks us
We fall, we crawl
But we don't call
Pride forbids us
The man in you is stoic
The woman in me stubborn

Grace lingers
Closing gaps
We touch each other
Until we mend.
*

We Are Not Dealing with Fractions

For TJH

We left fractions in the classroom
Poetry too
But not the poem

We started out halves, then wholes
Like numbers
Compound

Now we are even
Prime too
But not fractional

We've solved the equation and
Come to the value of variables
Separated by an equal sign
Practical math like counting
A-one, a-two, a-three, a-four
Like converting dollars into shillings
Pounds into francs
Consumer math — simple interest
Unit price with or without tax
Total estimate —
Love.
*

God and Man

In the stillness, in the quiet, in the solitude
In the chaos, in the raging storm
I see you
With me.

Enchanted, spirited
I reach out to you
Confused, lost, I run
How can I hide anywhere
When you are in everything?

The gift of silence you tell me to embrace
The joy of friendship across divides
The lonesome feeling deep down
The buoyant hope of better times.

You are God and man
I want you
I need you
Here and now
I am transformed thinking of you.
*

Portugal

Words grow cold
Time sits in the mirror
And when you look
Years stare
What happened?, you ask
When did I leave the race?

A tear, a tremor
All from the cracking place.
Frozen in October heat
Bones and all
A wish for chicken soup
Vegetable broth
Whatever can warm your inside
How did you arrive here?

The dreams turned to ashes
The colleagues, way ahead
Some dead.
What's left: mundane.

Suddenly you fall on your knees
Give thanks your knuckles still rattle with life
There is a voice inside you, a constant friend
A good job, a decent vacation
You have a phone, an email address, a computer
Above all you have a story
Miles to go there will be listeners
You've lived you.

Half through life you've gambled
You've changed, you've adapted

Life has beaten you to shape
You've not quit.
Giving thanks you call to ask
Are you holding on—friend?
*

For Those Who Grow Tired of Waiting

Faith makes the longing fulfilled,
Wait,
An absence that grows larger with years,
Louder with time.

Hope makes the heart strong,
Do not get tired,
Through uncertain moments and unsettled days,
Hold on like you would restrain a fart.

The wise say,
Happiness is not a station to arrive at,
But a manner of travelling,
Walk on, there's no age to the spirit.

Patience makes the unknown endurable,
Hold your neighbour's hand,
Lift up the feeble knees
Peace will come.
*